1 MONTH OF
FREE
READING

at
www.ForgottenBooks.com

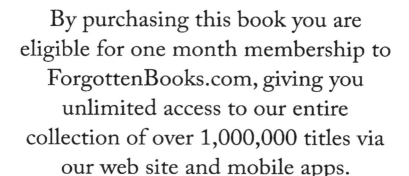

By purchasing this book you are eligible for one month membership to ForgottenBooks.com, giving you unlimited access to our entire collection of over 1,000,000 titles via our web site and mobile apps.

To claim your free month visit:
www.forgottenbooks.com/free36394

ISBN 978-0-484-30623-2
PIBN 10036394

This book is a reproduction of an important historical work. Forgotten Books uses
state-of-the-art technology to digitally reconstruct the work, preserving the original format
whilst repairing imperfections present in the aged copy. In rare cases, an imperfection in
the original, such as a blemish or missing page, may be replicated in our edition. We do,
however, repair the vast majority of imperfections successfully; any imperfections that
remain are intentionally left to preserve the state of such historical works.

For support please visit www.forgottenbooks.com

The Wisdom of the East Series

Edited by
L. CRANMER-BYNG
Dr. S. A. KAPADIA

THE CONDUCT OF LIFE

WISDOM OF THE EAST

THE CONDUCT OF LIFE

OR THE UNIVERSAL ORDER OF CONFUCIUS

A TRANSLATION OF ONE OF THE FOUR
CONFUCIAN BOOKS, HITHERTO KNOWN
AS THE DOCTRINE OF THE MEAN

BY KU HUNG MING, M.A. (EDIN.)

LONDON
JOHN MURRAY, ALBEMARLE STREET, W
1920

First Edition   .   .   .
Reprinted   .   .   .   . .
Reprinted   .   .   .   .

ALL RIGHTS RESERV

EDITORIAL NOTE

THE object of the Editors of this series is a very definite one. They desire above all things that, in their humble way, these books shall be the ambassadors of good-will and understanding between East and West—the old world of Thought and the new of Action. In this endeavour, and in their own sphere, they are but followers of the highest example in the land. They are confident that a deeper knowledge of the great ideals and lofty philosophy of Oriental thought may help to a revival of that true spirit of Charity which neither despises nor fears the nation of another creed and colour.

L. CRANMER-BYNG.
S. A. KAPADIA.

NORTHBROOK SOCIETY,
21 CROMWELL ROAD,
KENSINGTON, S.W.

INTRODUCTION

THE present volume is a translation of one of the four Confucian canonical books called the *Chung Yung*, which has been translated by Dr. Legge as the " Doctrine of the Mean." The Chinese word *Chung* means central—hence right, true, fair and square ; and *Yung* means common, ordinary—hence universal. The two Chinese words therefore mean the true, fair and square, universal standard of right ; in short, the common-sense of right.

The survival of the *Chung Yung* is attributed to K'ung Chi, the grandson of Confucius, who, fearing lest, as time went on, errors should creep into it, committed it to writing. The book, however, is not all made up of the sayings of Confucius, but contains much of K'ung Chi's own philosophy of life, founded more on insight and discernment than strict logic. Few works have been held in higher esteem by the intellectual classes of China. In the glowing words of Ch'êng, the master of

the greatest of all commentators, Chu Hsi:
" It first speaks of one principle ; it next spreads
this out, and embraces all things ; finally it re-
turns and gathers them all up under one principle.
Unroll it, and it fills the universe ; roll it up, and
it retires and lies hid in mysteriousness. The
relish of it is inexhaustible. The whole of it is
solid learning. When the skilful reader has ex-
plored it, he may carry it into practice all his life,
and will find that it cannot be exhausted."
Legge, the pioneer of English translation from the
Chinese classics, says of the *Chung Yung* that
" it gives the best account we have of the Confucian philosophy and morals, and will repay
careful study, and holds its place not only in
China, but in the wider sphere beyond it." The
Chung Yung is the third of the four great books
of Confucian teachings known as the " Four Shu."
The others are *The Lun Yü* or Analects, already
translated in The Wisdom of the East series by
Mr. Lionel Giles, the *Ta Hsüeh*, generally known
as *The Great Learning*, and attributed to Tsêng
Ts'an, a famous disciple of Confucius, and finally
the writings of Mencius, contained in seven
volumes.

The present book, together with the *Ta Hsüeh*,
translated by Dr. Legge as *The Great Learning*,
or, as it should be properly rendered, " Higher
Education," forms what may be called the Cate-
chism of the Confucian teaching. It was my

intention to publish these two books together. But I have not been able to bring my translation of the other book into a shape to satisfy the standard at which I aim. My object, after I have thoroughly mastered the meaning, is not only to reproduce the *matter*, but also the *manner* of the original. For, as Wordsworth says of all literature of really intrinsic value: " To be sure, it is the manner, but the matter always comes out of the manner." But to be able to reproduce the manner—what in literature is called the *style*—of the great and wise men of the past, one must try to put oneself in the same state of mind as that to which they attained—a thing one finds not easy, living in this modern world of the " civilisation of progress."

Most people now believe that the old order of things in China is passing away, and they hail the coming era of the new learning and of the civilisation of progress into this country. I for one do not believe that the old order of things in China can pass away. The reason is because I feel that the old order of things—the Chinese civilisation and Chinese social order—is a moral civilisation and a true social order, and cannot therefore, in the nature of things, pass away.

Now, it is the sense of responsibility in human conduct that makes not only civilisation but human society possible. Just think of a state of society where everybody disregards the feeling

of moral obligation in every relation of life. It
is impossible to imagine that such a state could
exist for one single hour or instant. Think, on
the other hand, of a state of society where everybody acts solely and in perfect accordance with
this sense of moral obligation. That would be
an ideal existence in which not only police but
all government would be unnecessary.

I say therefore that the Chinese civilisation is
a moral and true civilisation because in the first
place it not only recognises this moral obligation
as the fundamental basis of its social order, but
it makes the perfect attainment thereof in men
its sole aim. Consequently, in the social order,
the scheme of education, the method of government, and all social appliances have for their aim
and object to educate men to the sense of this
moral obligation ; and all those habits, tastes,
modes, and pursuits of life alone are encouraged
which are calculated to make it easy for men to
obey the moral obligation. In short, the ideal
goal which Chinese civilisation sets before mankind is not infinite happiness for everybody,
which means infinite self-indulgence for everybody, but the complete and perfect " realisation
of true moral being and moral order in mankind ;
so that the Universe shall become a cosmos
and all things can attain their full growth and
development."

I am well aware how very far the Chinese as

a nation and as individuals are at present from the realisation of the high ideal of their civilisation. But at the same time I think it right to say here that even now, looking upon the present demoralised state of things in China, the Chinese civilisation, if one would take the trouble to interpret and look into the inside of facts, cannot be considered a failure. If you judge a civilisation by the extent to which men of means living under that civilisation can enjoy themselves, then the Chinese civilisation·is certainly a failure. But if you judge a civilisation by the standard of strength and effectiveness of the sense of moral obligation in the nation living under that civilisation, then I think I can show that the Chinese civilisation even now is not a failure, but, on the contrary, a wonderful success.

Now, it is well known that in many parts of China at the present moment the greater portion of the population is living on the verge of starvation. It is also well known, or at least should be known, that the local authorities in China have no police, or any military force worth speaking of, to keep order. Nevertheless I think it can be shown that, taking the same area and size of population in any of the worst parts of these famine-stricken districts, there will be found there a smaller ratio of lawlessness, breaches of public order and crime than is to be found, say, in the wealthy and prosperous foreign model settlement of Shanghai, where there is a police force costing half a million taels a year. The Rev. Arthur Smith says : " The answer to Confucianism is China." I reply : Yes, the answer to Confucianism is China, only I say, you must look at China from the essential, moral side, and not merely from the electric-light side.

Indeed, if anything more is needed to prove what I have said, that the Chinese civilisation is a wonderful success, this one fact alone should prove it beyond any doubt or cavil : that notwithstanding the present demoralised state of the public services and the hunger-stricken condition of the people, the Chinese Government is still able to keep its public engagements with the foreign Powers for the Boxer indemnity. For what force is this upon which the mandarins in China depend, to make each unit of these four hundred millions hungry people in China pay up for a debt with which they individually have had nothing to do ? This force in China is not police or physical force. It is the force of the highly developed, law-abiding instinct of the Chinese people. Whence comes this instinct which is now standing so well the test and strain of present conditions ? It comes from a strong sense of moral obligation. But whence do the Chinese obtain this ? The answer is : from Chinese civilisation. I say, therefore, that Chinese civilisation is a wonderful success.

In the following translation then this idea of moral obligation, which forms the basis of human conduct and social order in the scheme of the Chinese civilisation, will be explicitly set forth. There is of course no " new learning " in all this, but what is better, there is *true* learning in it. The enunciation of it in some form or other is to be found in the best literature of every nation that has ever had a civilisation ; and what is most remarkable, as I have shown in the notes I have appended to the translation of the text, the enunciation in the same form and language as it is in this book, written two thousand years ago, is to be found in the latest writings of the best and greatest thinkers of modern Europe.

KU HUNG-MING.

THE CONDUCT OF LIFE

I

THE ordinance of God is what we call the law of our being. To fulfil the law of our being is what we call the moral law. The moral law when reduced to a system is what we call religion.

The moral law is a law from whose operation we cannot for one instant in our existence escape. A law from which we may escape is not the moral law. Wherefore it is that the moral man watches diligently over what his eyes cannot see and is in fear and awe of what his ears cannot hear.

There is nothing more evident than that which cannot be seen by the eyes and nothing more palpable than that which cannot be

14

perceived by the senses. Wherefore the moral man watches diligently over his secret thoughts.

Keep thy heart with all diligence, for out of it are the issues of life.—PROV. iv. 23.

When the passions, such as joy, anger, grief, and pleasure, have not awakened, that is our true self, or moral being. When these passions awaken and each and all attain due measure and degree, that is the moral order. Our true self or moral being is the great reality (*lit.* great root) of existence, and moral order is the universal law in the world.

When true moral being and moral order are realised, the universe then becomes a cosmos and all things attain their full growth and development.

II

Confucius remarked: "The life of the moral man is an exemplification of the universal moral order. The life of the vulgar person, on the other hand, is a contradiction of the universal moral order.

" The moral man's life is an exemplification of the universal order, because he is a moral person who unceasingly cultivates his true self or moral being. The vulgar person's life is a contradiction of the universal order, because he is a vulgar person who in his heart has no regard for, or fear of, the moral law."

The fool hath said in his heart, There is no God.

III

Confucius remarked : " To find the central clue to our moral being which unites us to the universal order, that indeed is the highest human attainment. People are seldom capable of it for long."

IV

Confucius remarked : " I know now why there is no real moral life. The wise mistake moral law for something higher than what it really is ; and the foolish do not know enough what moral law really is. I know now why the moral law is not understood. The noble natures want to live too high, high above their moral ordinary self; and ignoble natures do not live high enough, *i.e.*, not up to their moral ordinary true self."

" There is no one who does not eat and drink. But few there are who really know the taste of what they eat and drink."

Goethe says : " O needless strictness of morality while Nature in her kindly way trains us to all that we require to be ! O strange demand of society which first perplexes and misleads us, then asks of us more than Nature herself ! "— The moral law is the law of our moral nature ; and moral nature, what we call our moral being, is nothing else but our true or ordinary self.

V

Confucius remarked : " There is in the world now really no moral social order at all."

The word *tao* here means the moral law finding its expression in social order. Confucius in his time, as Carlyle and

2

Ruskin in modern Europe, considered the world to have gone
on a wrong track; the ways of men and constitution of
society to be radically wrong.

VI.

Confucius remarked : " There was the Emperor Shun. He was perhaps what . may be
considered a truly great intellect. Shun had a
natural curiosity of mind and he loved to inquire
into near facts (literally ' near words,' meaning
here ordinary topics of conversation in every-day
life). He looked upon evil merely as something
negative ; and he recognised only what was good
as having a positive existence. Taking the two
extremes of negative and positive, he applied
the mean between the two extremes in his judgment, employment and dealings with people.
This was the characteristic of Shun's great
intellect."

What is here said of the Emperor Shun in ancient China
may be also said of the two greatest intellects in modern
Europe—Shakespeare and Goethe. The greatness of Shakespeare's intellect is to be seen in this : that in all his plays
there is not one essentially bad man. Seen through Shakespeare's intellect, such a monster of wickedness of the popular
imagination as King Richard the Hunchback, becomes not
a villain who makes "damnable faces," not even a really

despicably bad man, but, on the contrary, a brave heroic soul who is driven by his strong, ill-regulated, vindictive passions to awful acts of cruelty and finally himself to a tragic end.

Goethe elsewhere says : "What we call evil in human nature is merely a defective or incomplete development, a deformity or malformation—absence or excess of some moral quality rather than anything positively evil."

VII

Confucius remarked : " Men all say ' We are wise ' ; but when driven forward and taken in a net, a trap, or a pitfall, there is not one who knows how to find a way of escape. Men all say, ' We are wise ' ; but in finding the true central clue and balance in their moral being (*i.e.*, their normal, ordinary, true self) and following the line of conduct which is in accordance with it, they are not able to keep it for a round month."

In other words, before a man undertakes to carry out any scheme of reform in the state of his affairs or the affairs of a nation, he must first of all take in hand the reform of his or their own being. In short, moral reform must precede all and every other reform.

VIII

Confucius remarked of his favourite disciple, Yen Hui: "Hui was a man who all his life sought the central clue in his moral being, and when he got hold of one thing that was good he embraced it with all his might and never lost it again."

As the Emperor Shun in the text above is the type of the intellectual nature, true representative of what Mr. Matthew Arnold calls Hellenism, so Yen Hui here is the type of the moral, emotional, or religious nature, true representative of what Mr. Arnold calls Hebraism.

IX.

Confucius remarked: "A man may be able to renounce the possession of kingdoms and empire, be able to spurn the honours and emoluments of office, be able to trample upon bare, naked weapons: with all that he shall not be able to find the central clue in his moral being."

The word chün in the text above, literally "even, equally divided," is here used as a verb meaning "to be indifferent to," hence to renounce. As in the chapter immediately following that in which he describes the characteristics of the great intellect, the writer of this book shows the conceit and uselessness of the half intellect, the characteristics of false Hellenism ; so in the present chapter following the above in which he gives the true type of Hebraism, he here again quotes another saying of Confucius showing the characteristics of false Hebraism, the evils and abuses resulting from the loss of balance on the moral, emotional, or religious side.

X

Tzu-lu asked what constituted force of character.

Confucius said : " Do you mean force of character of the people of the southern countries or force of character of the people of the northern countries ; or do you mean force of character in an absolute sense ? To be patient and gentle, ready to teach, returning not evil for evil : that is the force of character of the people of the southern countries. It is the ideal of the moral man."

Gentle unto all men, apt to teach, patient, in meekness instructing those that oppose themselves.—2 Tim. ii. 24, 25.

" To lie under arms and meet death without

regret : that is the force of character of the
people of the northern countries. It is the ideal
of the brave man."

"But force of character in an absolute sense
is another thing. Wherefore the man with the
true force of moral character is one who is easy
and accommodating and yet without weakness
or indiscrimination. How unflinchingly firm he
is in his strength ! He is independent without
any bias. How unflinchingly firm he is in his
strength ! When there is moral social order in
the country, if he enters public life he does not
change from what he was when in retirement.
When there is no moral social order in the country
he holds on his way without changing even unto
death. How unflinchingly firm he is in his
strength ! "

XI

Confucius remarked : "There are men who seek
for some abstruse meaning in religion and
philosophy and live a life singular in order
that they may leave a name to posterity. This
is what I never would do."

"There are again good men who try to live
in conformity with the moral law, but who, when

they have gone half way, throw it up.   I never could give it up."

" Lastly, there are truly moral men who unconsciously live a life in entire harmony with the universal moral order and who live unknown to the world and unnoticed of men without any concern.   It is only men of holy, divine natures who are capable of this."

XII

The moral law is to be found everywhere, and yet it is a secret.

The simple intelligence of ordinary men and women of the people may understand something of the moral law ; but in its utmost reaches there is something which even the wisest and holiest of men cannot understand. The ignoble natures of ordinary men and women of the people may be able to carry out the moral law ; but in its utmost reaches even the wisest and holiest of men cannot live up to it.

Great as the Universe is, man with the infinite moral nature in him is never satisfied.   For there is nothing so great but the mind of the moral man can conceive of something still greater which nothing in the world can hold.   There is nothing so small but the mind of moral man can conceive of something still smaller which nothing in the world can split.

The Book of Songs says :

" The hawk soars to the heavens above and fishes dive to the depths below."

That is to say, there is no place in the highest heavens above nor in the deepest waters below where the moral law does not reign.

Emerson says : " The moral law lies at the centre of Nature and radiates to the circumference.   It is the pith and marrow of every substance, every relation and every process."

The moral law takes its rise in the relation between man and woman ; but in its utmost reaches it reigns supreme over heaven and earth.

Morality begins with Sex.   Students of German literature may remember Faust's confession of faith to Margaret :

" Lifts not the Heaven its dome above ?
   Doth not the firm-set Earth beneath us lie ?
And beaming tenderly with looks of love,
   Climb not the everlasting stars on high ?

Do we not gaze into each other's eyes ?
  Nature's impenetrable agencies,
Are they not thronging on thy heart and brain,
  Viewless, invisible to mortal ken,
Around thee weaving their mysterious chain ?
  Fill thence thy heart, how large soe'er it be,
And in the feeling, when thou utterly art blest,
  Then call it what thou wilt—
Call it Bliss ! Heart ! Love ! God ! ''

XIII

Confucius remarked : " The moral law is not something away from the actuality of human life. When men take up something away from the actuality of human life as the moral law, that is not the moral law."

The Kingdom of God is within you.

The Book of Songs says :

" In hewing an axe handle, the pattern is not far off."

" Thus, when we take an axe handle in our hand to hew the other and glance from one to the other there is still some distance between them as compared with the relation between the moral law and the man himself. Wherefore the moral man in dealing with men appeals to the common human nature and changes the manner of their lives and nothing more.

" When a man carries out the principles of conscientiousness and reciprocity he is not far from the moral law. What you do not wish others should do unto you, do not do unto them.

" There are four things in the moral life of a man, not one of which I have been able to carry out in my life. To serve my father as I would expect my son to serve me : that I have not been able to do. To serve my sovereign as I would expect a minister under me to serve me : that I have not been able to do. To act towards my elder brother as I would expect my younger brother to act towards me : that I have not been able to do. To be the first to behave towards friends as I would expect them to behave towards me : that I have not been able to do.

" In the discharge of the ordinary duties of life and in the exercise of care in ordinary conversation, whenever there is shortcoming, never fail to strive for improvement, and when there is much to be said, always say less than what is necessary ; words having respect to actions, and actions having respect to words. Is it not just this thorough genuineness and absence of pretence which characterises the moral man ? "

XIV

The moral man conforms himself to his life circumstances ; he does not desire anything outside of his position.

Finding himself in a position of wealth and honour, he lives as becomes one living in a position of wealth and honour. Finding himself in a position of poverty and humble circumstances, he lives as becomes one living in a position of poverty and humble circumstances. Finding himself in uncivilized countries, he lives as becomes one living in uncivilized countries. Finding himself in circumstances of danger and difficulty, he acts according to what is required of a man under such circumstances. In one word, the moral man can find himself in no situation in life in which he is not master of himself.

In a high position he does not domineer over his subordinates. In a subordinate position he does not court the favours of his superiors. He puts in order his own personal conduct and seeks nothing from others ; hence he has no complaint to make. He complains not against God nor rails against men.

Thus it is that the moral man lives out the even tenor of his life, calmly waiting for the appointment of God, whereas the vulgar person takes to dangerous courses, expecting the uncertain chances of luck.

Confucius remarked : " In the practice of archery we have something resembling the principle in a moral man's life. When the archer misses the centre of the target he turns round and seeks for the cause of his failure within himself."

XV

The moral life of man may be likened to travelling to a distant place: one must start from the nearest stage. It may also be likened to ascending a height : one must begin from the lowest step.

The Book of Songs says :

" When wives and children and their sires are
    one,
  'Tis like the harp and lute in unison,

When brothers live in concord and at
  peace
The strain of harmony shall never cease.
The lamp of happy union lights the home,
And bright days follow when the children
  come."

Confucius, commenting on the above, remarked : " In such a state of things what more
satisfaction can parents have ? "

In what follows, I have ventured to alter the sequence of
the sections as they stand in the original text.   The following
section stands in the original as Section **XX.**

XVI.

Duke Ai (ruler of Confucius' native state)
asked what constituted good government.

Confucius replied : " The principles of good
government of the Emperors Wen and Wu
are abundantly illustrated in the records
preserved.   When the men are there, good
government will flourish, but when the men are
gone, good government decays and becomes
extinct.

" With the right men the growth of good

government is as rapid as the growth of vegetation is in the right soil. Indeed, good government is like a fast-growing plant.

" The conduct of government, therefore, depends upon the men. The right men are obtained by the ruler's personal character. To put in order his personal character, the ruler must use the moral law. To put in order the moral law, the ruler must use the moral sense.

" The moral sense is the characteristic attribute of man. To feel natural affection for those nearly related to us is the highest expression of the moral sense. The sense of justice is the recognition of what is right and proper. To honour those who are worthier than ourselves is the highest expression of the sense of justice. The relative degrees of natural affection we ought to feel for those who are nearly related to us and the relative grades of honour we ought to show to those worthier than ourselves : these are that which gives rise to the forms and distinctions in social life. For unless social inequalities_have a true and moral basis, government of the people is an impossibility."

According to Confucius, here, the basis of social inequalities rests upon two moral foundations, viz., the moral sense, the highest expression of which is natural affection—the feeling of love which all men feel for those nearly related to them— and the sense of justice, the highest expression of which is hero-worship—the feeling of respect and submission which all men feel for those worthier than themselves. In the family, natural affection makes submission easy, and in the state, hero-worship makes subordination natural and proper. But in Europe the plea for the justification of social inequalities is interests. The people are told to submit to the constituted authorities and to put up with social inequalities because it is to their interest to do so ; for if they allow the anarchists to have their way and destroy social inequalities, the evils which will result from this will be worse than the evils of social inequalities.

" Therefore it is necessary for a man of the governing class to set about regulating his personal conduct and character. In considering how to regulate his personal conduct and character it is necessary for him to do his duties towards those nearly related to him. In considering how to do his duties towards those nearly related to him it is necessary for him to understand the nature and organisation of human society. In considering the nature and organisation of human society it is necessary for him to understand the laws of God.

" The duties of universal obligation are five, and the moral qualities by which they are carried out are three. The duties are those between ruler and subject ; between father and son ; between husband and wife ; between elder brother and younger ; and those in the intercourse between friends. These are the five duties of universal obligation. Intelligence, moral character and courage : these are the three universally recognised moral qualities of man. It matters not in what way men come to the exercise of these moral qualities, the result is one and the same.

" Some men are born with the knowledge of these moral qualities ; some acquire it as the result of education ; some acquire it as the result of hard experience. But when the knowledge is acquired, it comes to one and the same thing. Some exercise these moral qualities naturally and easily ; some because they find it advantageous to do so ; some with effort and difficulty. But when the achievement is made it comes to one and the same thing."

Confucius went on to say : " Love of knowledge is the characteristic of men of intellectual character. Strenuous attention to conduct is the characteristic of men of moral character. Sensitiveness to shame is the characteristic of men of courage or heroic character.*

" When a man understands the nature and use of these three moral qualities, he will then understand how to put in order his personal conduct and character. When a man understands

* See note on Section VIII, p. 20.

how to put in order his personal conduct and character, he will understand how to govern men. When a man understands how to govern men, he will then understand how to govern nations and empires.

For every one called to the government of nations and empires there are nine cardinal directions to be attended to :

1. Putting in order his personal conduct.
2. Honouring worthy men.
3. Cherishing affection for, and doing his duty towards, his kindred.
4. Showing respect to the high ministers of state.
5. Identifying himself with the interests and welfare of the whole body of public officers.
6. Showing himself as a father to the common people:
7. Encouraging the introduction of all useful arts.
8. Showing tenderness to strangers from far countries.
9. Taking interest in the welfare of the princes of the Empire.

" When the ruler pays attention to putting in order his personal conduct, there will be respect for the moral law. When the ruler honours

worthy men, he will not be deceived. ' When the
ruler cherishes affection for his kindred, there
will be no disaffection among the members of his
family.   When the ruler shows respect to the
high ministers of state, he will not make mistakes.
When the ruler identifies himself with the interests and welfare of the body of public officers,
there will be a strong spirit of loyalty among the
gentlemen of the country.   When the ruler becomes a father to the common people, the mass
of the people will exert themselves for the good
of the state.   When the ruler encourages the
introduction of all useful arts, there will be suffi-
ciency of wealth and revenue in the country.
When the ruler shows tenderness to the strangers
from far countries, people from all quarters of the
world will flock to the country.   When the ruler
takes interest in the condition and welfare of the
princes of the empire, he will inspire awe and
respect for his authority throughout the whole
world.

" By attending to the cleanliness and purity
of his person and to the propriety and dignity of
his dress, and in every word and act permitting
nothing which is contrary to good taste and
decency : that is how the ruler puts in order his
personal conduct.

" By banishing all flatterers and keeping away
from the society of women ; holding in low esti-
mation possession of worldly goods, but valuing

moral qualities in men : that is how the ruler gives encouragement to worthy men. By raising them to high places of honour and bestowing ample emoluments for their maintenance ; sharing and sympathising with their tastes and opinions : that is how the ruler inspires love for his person among the members of his family. By extending the powers of their functions and allowing them discretion in the employment of their subordinates : that is how the ruler gives encouragement to the high ministers of state. By dealing loyally and punctually with them in all engagements which he makes with them and allowing a liberal scale of pay : that is how the ruler gives encouragement to men in the public service. By strictly limiting the time of their service and making all imposts as light as possible : that is how the ruler gives encouragement to the mass of the people. By ordering daily inspection and monthly examination and rewarding each according to the degree of his workmanship : that is how the ruler encourages the artisan class. By welcoming them when they come and giving them protection when they go, commending what is good in them and making allowance for their ignorance : that is how the ruler shows tenderness to strangers from far countries. By restoring lines of broken succession and reviving extinguished states, putting down anarchy and disorder wherever they are found, and giving support to the weak against the strong, fixing stated times for their attendance and the attendance of their envoys at court, loading them with presents when they leave, while exacting little from them in the way of contribution when they come : that is how the ruler takes interest in the welfare of the princes of the empire.

" For every one who is called to the government of nations and empire, these are the nine cardinal directions to be attended to ; and there is only one way by which they can be carried out. In all matters success depends on preparation ; without preparation there will always be failure. When what is to be said is previously determined, there will be no breakdown. When what is to be done is previously determined, there will be no difficulty in carrying it out. When a line of conduct is previously determined, there will be no occasion for vexation. When general principles are previously determined, there will be no perplexity to know what to do.

" If those in authority have not the confidence of those under them, government of the people is an impossibility. There is only one way to gain confidence for one's authority. If a man is not trusted by his friends, he will not gain the confidence for his authority. There is only one way to be trusted by one's friends. If a man does not command the obedience of the members of his

family, he will not be trusted by his friends.
There is only one way to command the obedience
of the members of one's family. If a man, looking into his own heart, is not true to himself,
he will not command the obedience of the
members of his family. There is only one way
for a man to be true to himself. If he does
not know what is good, a man cannot be true
to himself."

"Truth is the law of God. Acquired truth is
the law of man."

"He who intuitively apprehends truth is one
who, without effort, hits what is right, and without thinking understands what he wants to
khow; whose life is easily and naturally in
harmony with the moral law. Such a one is what
we call a saint or a man of divine nature. He
who acquires truth is one who finds out what is
good and holds fast to it.

"In order to acquire truth, it is necessary to
obtain a wide and extensive knowledge of what
has been said and done in the world; critically to
inquire into it; carefully to ponder over it;
clearly to sift it; and earnestly to carry it
out."

"It matters not what you learn, but when you
once learn a thing you must never give it up
until you have mastered it. It matters not what
you inquire into, but when you inquire into a
thing you must never give it up until you have

thoroughly understood it. It matters not what
you try to think out, but when you once try to
think out a thing you must never give it up until
you have got what you want. It matters not
what you try to sift out, but when you once try
to sift out a thing, you must never give it up until
you have sifted it out clearly and distinctly. It
matters not what you try to carry out, but when
you once try to carry out a thing you must never
give it up until you have done it thoroughly and
well. If another man succeed by one effort, you
will use a hundred efforts. If another man
succeed by ten efforts, you will use a thousand
efforts."

"Let a man really proceed in this manner,
and, though dull, he will surely become intelligent ; though weak, he will surely become
strong."

XVII

Confucius remarked : "The Emperor Shun
might perhaps be considered in the highest sense
of the word a pious man. In moral qualities
he was a saint. In dignity of office he was
the ruler of the empire. In wealth all that
the wide world contained belonged to him.

After his death his spirit was sacrificed to in the ancestral temple, and his children and grandchildren preserved the sacrifice for long generations.

" Thus it is that he who possesses great moral qualities will certainly attain to corresponding high position ; to corresponding great prosperity ; to corresponding great name ; to corresponding great age.

" For God in giving life to all created things is surely bountiful to them according to their qualities. Hence the tree that is full of life He fosters and sustains, while that which is ready to fall He cuts off and destroys."

The law of the survival of the fittest is here announced two thousand years ago. But Confucius' interpretation of this law is different from the modern interpretation. The survival of the fittest means, not the survival of the most brutally strong, but the survival of the morally fittest.

The Book of Songs says :

" That great and noble Prince displayed
   The sense of right in all he wrought ;
Adjusting justly, grade by grade,
   The spirit of his wisdom swayed
Peasant and peer ; the crowd, the court.

So Heav'n, that crowned his sires, restored
  The countless honours they had known ;
For Heav'n aye keepeth watch and ward,
  And through the son renews the throne."

" It is therefore true that he who possesses exceedingly great moral qualities will certainly receive the divine call to the Imperial throne."

XVIII

Confucius remarked : " The man perhaps who enjoyed the most perfect happiness was the Emperor Wen. For father he had a remarkable man, the Emperor Chi, and for son also a remarkable man, the Emperor Wu. His father laid the foundation of his House and his son carried it on. The Emperor Wu, continuing the great work begun by his ancestor the great Emperor, his grandfather Chi and his father the Emperor Wen, had only to buckle on his armour and the Empire at once came to his possession.

" The Emperor Wen was a no less distinguished man. In dignity of office he was the ruler of the Empire ; in wealth all that the wide world contained belonged to him. After his death his spirit was sacrificed to in the ancestral temple, and his children and grandchildren preserved the sacrifice for long generations.

" The Emperor Wen never actually ascended the throne. But his son, the Duke of Chow, ascribed the achievement of founding the Imperial House equally to the moral qualities of the Emperors Wen and Wu. He carried the Imperial title up to the Great Emperor (Wen's grandfather) and the Emperor Chi (Wen's father). He sacrificed to all the past reigning dukes of the House with imperial honours."

This rule is now universally observed from the reigning princes and nobles to the gentlemen and common people. In the case where the father is a noble and the son is a simple gentleman, the father, when he dies, is buried with the honours of a noble, but sacrificed to as a simple gentleman. In the case where the father is a simple gentleman and the son a noble, the father, when he dies, is buried as a simple gentleman, but sacrificed to with the honours of a nobleman. The rule for one year of mourning for relatives is binding up to the rank of a noble, but the rule for three years of mourning for parents is binding for all up to the Emperor. In mourning for parents there is only one rule, and no distinction is made between noble and plebeian.

XIX

Confucius remarked : " The Emperor Wu and his brother, ' the Duke of Chow, were indeed eminently pious men. Now, true filial piety consists in successfully carrying out the unfinished work of our forefathers and transmitting their achievements to posterity.

" In spring and autumn they repaired and put in order the ancestral temple ; arranged the sacrificial vessels, exhibited the regalia and heirlooms of the family, and presented the appropriate offerings of the season.

" The principle in the order of precedence in the ceremonies of worship in the ancestral temple is, in the first place, to arrange the members of the family according to descent. Ranks are next considered, in order to give recognition to the principle of social distinction. Services rendered are next considered as a recognition of distinction in moral worth. In the general banquet those below take precedence of those above in pledging the company, in order to show that consideration is shown to the meanest. In

AS OUR FATHERS HAVE DONE

conclusion, a separate feast is given to the elders, in order to recognise the principle of seniority according to age."

To gather in the same places where our fathers before us have gathered ; to perform the same ceremonies which they before us have performed ; to play the same music which they before us have played ; to pay respect to those whom they honoured ; to love those who were dear to them— in fact, to serve them now dead as if they were living, and now departed as if they were still with us : this is the highest achievement of true filial piety.

The performance of sacrifices to Heaven and Earth is meant for the service of God. The performance of ceremonies in the ancestral temple is meant for the worship of ancestors. If one only understood the meaning of the sacrifices to Heaven and Earth, and the signification of the services in ancestral worship, it would be the easiest thing to govern a nation.

XX

Confucius remarked : " The power of spiritual forces in the Universe—how active it is everywhere ! Invisible to the eyes, and impalpable to the senses, it is inherent in all things, and nothing can escape its operation."

It is the fact that there are these forces which make men in all countries fast and purify themselves, and with solemnity of dress institute services of sacrifice and religious worship. Like the rush of mighty waters, the presence of unseen Powers is felt : sometimes above us, sometimes around us.

In the Book of Songs it is said :

> " The presence of the Spirit :
>   It cannot be surmised,
>   Inspiring fear and awe."

Such is the evidence of things invisible that it is impossible to doubt the spiritual nature of man.

XXI

The intelligence which comes from the direct apprehension of truth is intuition. The apprehension of truth which comes from the exercise of intelligence is the result of education. Where there is truth, there is intelligence; where there is intelligence, there is truth.

XXII

It is only he, in the world, who possesses absolute truth who can get to the bottom of the law of his being. He who is able to get to the bottom of the law of his being will be able to get to the bottom of the law of being of other men. He who is able to get to the bottom of the law of being of men will be able to get to the bottom of the laws of physical nature. He who is able to get to the bottom of the laws of physical nature will be able to influence the forces of creation of the Universe. He who can influence the forces of creation of the Universe is one with the Powers of the Universe.

XXIII

The next order of the process of man's mind is to attain to the apprehension of a particular branch of knowledge. In every particular branch of knowledge there is truth. Where there is truth, there is substance. Where there is sub-stance, there is reality. Where there is reality, there is intelligence. Where there is intelligence, there is power. Where there is power, there is influence. Where there is influence, there is creative power. It is only he who possesses absolute truth in the world who can create.

XXIV

It is an attribute of the possession of absolute truth to be able to foreknow. When a nation or family is about to flourish, there are sure to be lucky omens. When a nation or family is about to perish, there are sure to be signs and prodigies. These things manifest themselves in the instruments of divination and in the agitation of the human body. When happiness or calamity is about to come, it can be known beforehand. When it is good, it can be known beforehand. When it is evil, it can also be known beforehand. Therefore he who possesses absolute truth is like a spiritual being.

XXV

Truth means the realisation of our being ; and moral law means the law of our being. Truth is the beginning and end (the substance) of existence. Without truth there is no existence. It is for this reason that the moral man values truth.

Truth is not only the realisation of our own being: it is that by which things outside of us have an existence. The realisation of our being is moral sense. The realisation of things outside of us is intellect. These, moral sense and intellect, are the powers or faculties of our being. They combine the inner or subjective and outer or objective use of the power of the mind. Therefore with truth everything done is right.

XXVI

Thus absolute truth is indestructible. Being indestructible, it is eternal. Being eternal, it is self-existent. Being self-existent, it is infinite. Being infinite, it is vast and deep. Being vast and deep, it is transcendental and intelligent.

It is because it is vast and deep that it contains all existence. It is because it is transcendental and intelligent that it embraces all existence. It is because it is infinite and eternal that it fills all existence. In vastness and depth it is like the Earth. In transcendental intelligence it is like Heaven. Infinite and eternal, it is Infinitude itself.

Such being the nature of absolute truth, it manifests itself without being evident; it produces effects without action ; it accomplishes its ends without being conscious.

The principle in the course and operation of nature may be summed up in one word : it exists for its own sake without any double or ulterior motive. Hence the way in which it produces things is unfathomable.

Nature is vast, deep, high, intelligent, infinite, and eternal. The heaven appearing before us is only this bright, shining spot ; but when taken in its immeasurable extent, the sun, moon, stars, and constellations are suspended in it, and all things are embraced under it. The earth, appearing before us, is but a handful of soil ; but taken in all its breadth and depth, it sustains mighty Himalayas without feeling their weight ; rivers and seas dash against it without causing it to leak. The mountain appearing before us is only a mass of rock ; but taken in all the vastness of its size, grass and vegetation grow upon it, birds and beasts dwell on it, and treasures of precious stones are found in it.   The water appearing before us is but a ladleful of liquid ; but taken in all its unfathomable depths, the largest crustaceans, fishes, and reptiles are produced in them, and all useful products abound in them.

In the Book of Songs it is said :

" The ordinance of God,
How inscrutable it is and goes on for ever."

That is to say, this is the attribute of God. It is again said :

" How excellent it is,
The moral perfection of King Wen."

That is to say, this is the characteristic of the nobleness of the Emperor Wen.   Moral perfection also never dies.

XXVII

Oh, how great is the divine moral law in man !   Vast and illimitable, it gives birth and

4

life to all created things. It towers high up to the very heavens. How wonderful and great it is ! All the institutions of human society and civilisation—laws, customs, and usages—have their origin there. All these institutions wait for the man before they can be put into practice. Hence it is said : Unless there be highest moral power, the highest moral law cannot be realised.

Wherefore the moral man, while honouring the greatness and power of his moral nature, yet does not neglect inquiry and pursuit of knowledge. While widening the extent of his knowledge, he yet seeks to attain utmost accuracy in the minutest details. While seeking to understand the highest things, he yet lives a plain, ordinary life in accordance with the moral order. Going over what he has already acquired, he keeps adding to it new knowledge. Earnest and simple, he respects and obeys the laws and usages of social life.

Therefore, when in a position of authority, he is not proud ; in a subordinate position, he is not insubordinate. When there is moral social order in the country, what he speaks will be of benefit to the nation ; and when there is no moral social order in the country his silence will ensure forbearance for himself.

In the Book of Songs it is said :

" With wisdom and good sense,
He guards his life from harm."

That is the description of the moral man.

Confucius remarked : " A man who is foolish, and yet is fond of using his own judgment ; who is in humble circumstances, and yet is fond of assuming authority ; who, while living in the present age, reverts to the ways of antiquity : such a man is one who will bring calamity upon himself."

To no one but the supreme head of the empire does it belong to disturb the established religious and social institutions, to introduce new forms of government, to change the form and use of language. At the present day throughout the empire carriage wheels all have the same standard form and size, all writing is written with the same characters, and in all the relations of life all recognise the same established principles.

Although a man may occupy the position of the supreme head of the empire, yet, unless he possesses the moral qualities fitting him for the task, he may not take upon himself to make changes in the established moral and religious institutions. Although one may possess the moral qualities fitting him for the task, yet, unless he occupies the position of the supreme head of the empire, he may not take upon himself to make changes in the established moral and religious institutions.

Confucius remarked : " I have tried to understand the moral and religious institutions of the Hsia dynasty, but what remains of those institutions in the present state of Ch'i is not sufficient to give me a clue. I have studied the moral and religious institutions of the Yin dynasty ; the remains of them are still preserved in the present state of Sung. I have studied the moral and religious institutions of the present Chow dynasty, which are now in use. In practice I follow the forms of the present Chow dynasty."

XXVIII

To attain to the sovereignty of the world, there are three important things necessary ; they may perhaps be summed up in one : blamelessness of life.

However excellent a system of moral truths

appealing to supernatural authority may be, it is not verifiable by experience; what is not verifiable by experience cannot command credence; and what cannot command credence the people will never obey. However excellent a system of moral truths appealing merely to worldly authority may be it does not command respect; what does not command respect cannot command credence; and what cannot command credence the people will never obey.

Therefore every system of moral laws must be based upon the man's own consciousness. It must be verified by the common experience of men. Examined into by comparing it with the teachings of acknowledged great and wise men of the past, there must be no divergence. Applying it to the operations and processes of nature in the physical universe, there must be no contradiction. Confronted with the spiritual powers of the universe a man must be able to maintain it without any doubt. He must be prepared to wait a hundred generations after him for the coming of a man of perfect divine nature to confirm it without any misgiving. The fact that he is able to confront the spiritual powers of the universe without any doubt, shows that he understands the will of God. The fact that he is prepared to wait a hundred generations after him for the man of perfect divine nature without any misgiving, shows that he understands the nature of man.

Wherefore it is that it is true of the really great moral man, that every act of his life becomes an example for generations; everything he does becomes a statute for generations, and every word he utters becomes a law for generations. Those who are far away and do not know him look up to him, while those who are near and know him do not reject him.

In the Book of Songs it is said:

" There they found no fault in him,
Here they ever welcome him;
Thus from day to day and night to night
They will perpetuate his praise! "

Thus a moral man, unless he realises this description of a man, can never obtain at once recognition of his moral qualities throughout the world.

XXIX

Confucius taught the truth originally handed down by the ancient Emperors Yao and Shun, and he adopted and perfected the system of moral laws established by the Emperors Wen and Wu. He showed that they harmonise with the divine order which governs the revolutions of the seasons in the Heaven above and that they fit in with the moral design which is to be seen in physical nature upon the Earth below.

These moral laws form one system with the laws by which Heaven and Earth support and contain, overshadow and canopy all things. These moral laws form the same system with the laws by which the seasons succeed each other and the sun and moon appear with the alternations of day and night. It is this same system of laws by which all created things are produced and develop themselves each in its order and system without injuring one another; that the operations of Nature take their course without conflict or confusion; the lesser forces flowing everywhere like river currents, while the great forces of Creation go silently and steadily on. It is this—one system running through all—that makes the Universe so impressively great.

XXX

It is only the man with the most perfect divine moral nature who is able to combine in himself quickness of apprehension, intelligence, insight, and understanding : qualities necessary for the exercise of command ; magnanimity, generosity, benignity and gentleness : qualities necessary for the exercise of patience ; originality, energy, strength of character and determination : qualities necessary for the exercise of endurance ; dignity, noble seriousness, order and regularity : qualities necessary for the exercise of self-respect ; grace, method, delicacy and lucidity : qualities necessary for the exercise of critical judgment.

Thus all-embracing and vast is the nature of such a man. Profound it is and inexhaustible, like a living spring of water, ever running out with life and vitality. All-embracing and vast, it is like Heaven. Profound and inexhaustible, it is like the abyss.

As soon as such a man shall make his appearance in the world, all people will reverence him. Whatever he says, all people will believe it. Whatever he does, all people will be pleased with it. Thus his fame and name will spread and fill all the civilised world, extending even to savage countries ; wherever ships and carriages reach ; wherever the labour and enterprise of man penetrate ; wherever the heavens overshadow and the earth sustains ; wherever sun and

THE KEY OF POWER

THE KEY OF POWER

moon shine; wherever frost and dew fall: all who have life and breath will honour and love him. Therefore we may say: " He is the equal of God."

XXXI

It is only he in this world who is possessed of absolute truth that can order and adjust the great relations of human society, fix the fundamental principles of morality, and understand the laws of creation of the Universe.

Now, where does such a man derive his power and knowledge except from himself? How all-absorbing his humanity! How unfathomable the depth of his mind! How infinitely grand and vast his divine nature! Who can understand such a nature except him who is gifted with the most perfect intelligence and endowed with the highest divine qualities of nature and mind?

XXXII

In the Book of Songs it is said:

" Over her brocaded robe,
    She wore a plain and simple dress,"

in that way showing her dislike of the loudness of its colour and magnificence. Thus the life of the moral man is unobtrusive and yet it grows more and more in significance ; whereas the life of the vulgar person is ostentatious, but it loses more and more in significance until it becomes nothingness.

The life of the moral man is plain, and yet not unattractive ; it is simple, and yet full of grace ; it is easy, and yet methodical. He knows that accomplishment of great things consists in doing little things well. He knows that great effects are produced by small causes. He knows the evidence and reality of what cannot be perceived by the senses. Thus he is enabled to enter into the world of ideas and morals.

In the Book of Songs it is said :

" How deep the fish may dive below,
And yet it is quite clearly seen."

Therefore the moral man must examine into his own heart and see that he has no cause for self-reproach, that he has no evil thought in his mind. Wherein the moral man is superior to other men consists even in that which is not seen by men.

In the Book of Songs it is said :

" In your secret chamber even you are judged ;
　　See you do nothing to blush for,
　　Though but the ceiling looks down upon you."

Therefore the moral man, even when he is not doing anything, is serious ; and, even when he does not speak, is truthful.

In the Book of Songs it is said :

" All through the solemn rite not a word was
　　spoken,
　　And yet all strife was banished from their
　　hearts."

Hence the moral man, without the inducement of rewards, is able to make the people good ; and without the show of anger, to awe them into fear more than if he had used the most dreadful instruments of punishment.

In the Book of Songs it is said :

" He makes no show of his moral worth,
　　Yet all the princes follow in his steps."

Hence the moral man, by living a life of simple truth and earnestness, alone can help to bring peace and order in the world.

In the Book of Songs it is said :

" I keep in mind the fine moral qualities which make no great noise or show."

Confucius remarked : " Among the means for the regeneration of mankind, those made with noise and show are of the least importance."

In another place in the Book of Songs it is said,

" His virtue is light as hair."

Still a hair is something material.   " The workings of Almighty God have neither sound nor smell."   There is nothing higher than that.

Printed by Hazell, Watson & Viney, Ld., London and Aylesbury, England.

THE WISDOM OF THE EAST SERIES

Edited by L. CRANMER-BYNG and Dr. S. A. KAPADIA

THE SERIES AND ITS PURPOSE

THIS Series has a definite object. It is, by means of the best Oriental literature—its wisdom, philosophy, poetry, and ideals—to bring together West and East in a spirit of mutual sympathy, goodwill, and understanding. From India, China, Japan, Persia, Arabia, Palestine, and Egypt these words of wisdom have been gathered.

NEW VOLUMES.

THE SECRET ROSE GARDEN OF SA'D UD DIN MAHMUD SHABISTARI. Rendered from the Persian, with an Introduction, by FLORENCE LEDERER.

THE RHYTHM OF LIFE. Based on the Philosophy of Lao-Tse. By HENRI BOREL. Translated by M. E. REYNOLDS.

INDIAN

THE RELIGION OF THE SIKHS. By DOROTHY FIELD.

BUDDHIST SCRIPTURES. A Selection Translated from the Pāli with Introduction by E. J. THOMAS, M.A.

THE HEART OF INDIA. Sketches in the History of Hindu Religion and Morals. By L. D. BARNETT, M.A., LITT.D., Professor of Sanskrit at University College, London.

BRAHMA-KNOWLEDGE: An Outline of the Philosophy of the Vedānta. As set forth by the Upanishads and by Sankara. By L. D. BARNETT, M.A., LITT.D., Professor of Sanskrit at University College, London.

THE BUDDHA'S "WAY OF VIRTUE." A Translation of the Dhammapada. By W. C. D. WAGISWARA and K. J. SAUNDERS, Members of the Royal Asiatic Societ   C   lon branch.

THE PATH OF LIGHT. Rendered for the first time into English from the Bodhi-charyāvatāra of Sānti-Deva. A Manual of Mahā-Yāna Buddhism. By L. D. BARNETT, M.A., LITT.D.

LEGENDS OF INDIAN BUDDHISM. Translated from " L'Introduction à l'Histoire du Buddhisme Indien " of Eugène Burnouf, with an Introduction by WINIFRED STEPHENS.

THE WAY OF THE BUDDHA. Selections from the Buddhist texts, together with the original Pāli, with Introduction by HERBERT BAYNES, M.R.A.S.

IRANIAN (Persian, Pehlvi, Zend, etc.)

THE DIWAN OF ZEB-UN-NISSA. The First Fifty Ghazals. Rendered from the Persian by MAGAN LAL and JESSIE DUNCAN WEST-BROOK. With an Introduction and Notes.

THE RUBA'IYÁT OF HÁFIZ. Translated with Introduction by SYED ABDUL MAJID, LL.D. Rendered into English Verse by L. CRANMER-BYNG.

THE SPLENDOUR OF GOD. Being Extracts from the Sacred Writings of the Bahais. With Introduction by ERIC HAMMOND.

THE TEACHINGS OF ZOROASTER, and the Philosophy of the Parsi Religion. Translated with Introduction by Dr S. A. KAPADIA, Lecturer, University College, London. 2nd Edition.

THE PERSIAN MYSTICS.
I. Jalálu'd-dín Rúmí. By F. HADLAND DAVIS.
II. Jámí. By F. HADLAND DAVIS.

THE BUSTÁN OF SA'DI. From the Persian. Translated with Introduction by A. HART EDWARDS.

SA'DI'S SCROLL OF WISDOM. By SHAIKH SA'DI. With Introduction by Sir ARTHUR N. WOLLASTON, K.C.I.E.
With Persian Script added.

THE ROSE GARDEN OF SA'DI. Selected and Rendered from the Persian with Introduction by L. CRANMER-BYNG.

ARABIC

THE POEMS OF MU'TAMID, KING OF SEVILLE. Rendered into English Verse by DULCIE LAWRENCE SMITH. With an Introduction.

ABU'L ALA, THE SYRIAN. By HENRY BAERLEIN.

THE ALCHEMY OF HAPPINESS. By AL GHAZZALI. Rendered into English by CLAUD FIELD.

THE RELIGION OF THE KORAN. With Introduction by Sir ARTHUR N. WOLLASTON, K.C.I.E.

ARABIAN WISDOM. Selections and Translations from the Arabic by JOHN WORTABET, M.D.

THE SINGING CARAVAN. Some Echoes of Arabian Poetry. By HENRY BAERLEIN.

THE DIWAN OF ABU'L-ALA. By HENRY BAERLEIN.

HEBREW

ANCIENT JEWISH PROVERBS. Compiled and Classified by A. COHEN, late Scholar of Emmanuel College, Cambridge.

THE WISDOM OF THE APOCRYPHA. With an Introduction by C. E. LAWRENCE, Author of "Pilgrimage," etc.

CHINESE

A FEAST OF LANTERNS. Rendered with an Introduction by L. CRANMER-BYNG, Author of "A Lute of Jade," "The Odes of Confucius," etc.

YANG CHU'S GARDEN OF PLEASURE. Translated from the Chinese by Professor ANTON FORKE. With an Introduction by H. CRANMER-BYNG.

TAOIST TEACHINGS. From the Mystical Philosophy of Lieh Tzŭ. Translated by LIONEL GILES, M.A.

A LUTE OF JADE. Being Selections from the Classical Poets of China. Rendered with an Introduction by L. CRANMER-BYNG. 2nd Edition.

THE CLASSICS OF CONFUCIUS.
 I. The Book of Odes (Shi-King).
   By L. CRANMER-BYNG.

 II. The Book of History (Shu-King).
   By W. GORN OLD.

THE SAYINGS OF CONFUCIUS. A new Translation of the greater part of the Confucian Analects, with Introduction and Notes by LIONEL GILES, M.A. (Oxon.), Assistant in the Department of Oriental Books and Manuscripts of the British Museum.

Confucius. A translation of one of the four Confucian Books, hitherto known as the Doctrine of the Mean. By Ku Hung Ming, M.A. (Edin.).

THE BOOK OF FILIAL DUTY. Translated from the Chinese of the Hsiao Ching by Ivan Chên, First Secretary to the Chinese Legation.

THE SAYINGS OF LAO TZŬ. From the Chinese. Translated with Introduction by Lionel Giles, of the British Museum.

MUSINGS OF A CHINESE MYSTIC. Selections from the Philosophy of Chuang Tzŭ. With Introduction by Lionel Giles, M.A. (Oxon.), Assistant at the British Museum.

THE FLIGHT OF THE DRAGON. An Essay on the Theory and Practice of Art in China and Japan, based on Original Sources. By Laurence Binyon.

JAPANESE

THE SPIRIT OF JAPANESE ART. By Yone Noguchi.

THE SPIRIT OF JAPANESE POETRY. By Yone Noguchi.

THE WAY OF CONTENTMENT. Translated from the Japanese of Kaibara Ekken by Ken Hoshino.

THE MASTER-SINGERS OF JAPAN. Being Verse Translations from the Japanese Poets. By Clara A. Walsh.

WOMEN AND WISDOM OF JAPAN. With Introduction by S. Takaish'.

EGYPTIAN

ANCIENT EGYPTIAN LEGENDS. By Margaret A. Murray.

THE BURDEN OF ISIS. Being the Laments of Isis and Nephthys. Translated from the Egyptian with an Introduction by James Teackle Dennis.

THE INSTRUCTION OF PTAH-HOTEP AND THE INSTRUCTION OF KE'GEMNI. The Oldest Books in the World. Translated from the Egyptian with Introduction and Appendix by Battiscombe Gunn.

Editorial Communications should be addressed to
The Editors of the Wisdom of the East Series,
50A, Albemarle Street, London, W.1

LONDON: JOHN MURRAY, ALBEMARLE STREET, W.

Lightning Source UK Ltd.
Milton Keynes UK
UKHW020759270219
338009UK00008B/1692/P